Inspiring
Women
Every Day

C000148186

March

THE PLACE OF REST

CAROL HERZIG

April

SHAMELESS

REBECCA BERRY

Plus... 'Be Inspired' article, and
Waverley Abbey pages.

MIX
Paper from responsible sources
FSC® C015900
www.fsc.org

WAVERLEY ABBEY
RESOURCES
Trading name of CWR

Carol Herzig

Carol is a language teacher and freelance writer with a passion for worship, reconciliation and church unity. Carol has worked with several Christian charities including CWR, particularly in editorial and hosting Bible Discovery weekends with her husband. Now in primary education, in her free time Carol enjoys walking, nature photography and learning to play jazz on her clarinet!

Rebecca Berry

Rebecca Berry was Lead Editor at CWR before becoming a mum to baby Lara and focusing more on writing. She is especially interested in theology and feminism, and loves working on anything that helps people understand more about the Bible, God and themselves. Rebecca lives in Surrey with her husband Chris, but a tiny piece of her heart will always belong to Suffolk..

The Place of Rest

CAROL HERZIG

We begin our month's readings by looking at one of the most action-packed days of Jesus' ministry. Jesus and His disciples do not have time to eat... that is, until late in the day, when Jesus miraculously multiplies loaves and fish – enough to feed 5,000 men and their families. Yet before this, we see Jesus' concern for His disciples: that they would eat – and get some rest.

When the Lord prompted me to write on 'The Place of Rest', the theme seemed fitting. Waiting for an operation that would fuse weight-bearing bones in my foot, I imagined that my recovery would include hours of stillness and reflection. I longed to experience God's deep rest and peace during an 'enforced Sabbath'. The reality was very different. For weeks I spent most of my time sleeping. And in my limited waking hours, daily activities took ten times as long. Hobbling on crutches and one leg for four months, I became frustrated that I wasn't experiencing the restful sabbatical I'd hoped for. A family crisis swiftly followed, my husband experienced a serious health scare, our church ended after 38 years, and then Covid-19 hit the world with its fearful and devastating consequences.

In the midst of what had become an immensely stressful, troubling time, the Lord clearly wanted *me* to learn how to live in His place of rest. So please join me this month on my journey: discovering how to enjoy resting in the Lord; to respond from a place of rest and with godly perspective when under pressure; and to grow in the Lord's peace, joy and thankfulness in our circumstances. I pray that you will find biblical insights, practical help and renewed hope.

Mark 6:7, 12–13,30–46

'Come with me by yourselves to a quiet place and get some rest.' (v31)

For prayer and reflection

Lord Jesus, You experienced constant demands and knew weariness and exhaustion. You invite me to come with You to rest. Teach me how to live from Your rest. Amen.

Rest **in creation**

**Genesis
1:24 –2:3**

'God blessed the
seventh day and
made it holy,
because on it He
rested from…
the work of
creating.' (2:3)

O n the sixth day, God surveyed His creation,
declaring it very good. Then He rested. Our
creator God never grows tired, nor slumbers or
sleeps, so He wasn't resting to renew His energy. The
Hebrew word for rest is *Shabbat*, meaning to cease or
stop. The prophet Isaiah links *Shabbat* (Sabbath) with
delight (Isa. 58:13). Did God cease His work of creation
to delight in all He'd made? Man and woman, created
on 'day six' (which theologians debate how literally
we should understand as a 24-hour period), began
life in a time of rest, enjoying the beauty of their new
surroundings with God. At the beginning of creation our
creator rested – and His rest is available to us today. Our
practice of Sabbath is rooted in this truth.

Rest is part of the cycle of life. At Mount Sinai, the
Lord commanded the Israelites, through Moses, to
observe a cycle of work and rest. Every seventh day was
to be a day of Sabbath, and every seventh year the land
was to lie fallow. Rest periods are essential for nature.
Deciduous trees may be dormant in winter, but their
roots continue to deepen and strengthen. Since the
Lord established this cycle of work and rest at the dawn
of creation, how important is it for us in our often non-
stop lives?

In Hebrews we read: 'There remains, then, a Sabbath-
rest for the people of God: for anyone who enters
God's rest also rests from their works, just as God did
from His' (Heb. 11:9–10). The writer then challenges us
to 'make every effort to enter that rest' (Heb. 3:9–11).
Next Monday, we'll consider how Christ's death and
resurrection have made this possible.

**For prayer
and reflection**

**Lord, help me to
examine the
priority I give to
rest. Jesus lived
from Your Sabbath
rest, and I want to
learn from His
example. Teach me,
this month, I pray.
Amen.**

The **holy** day of rest

Today we are reading from the Ten Commandments, ten foundational sayings spoken by God to Moses for the Israelites journeying to possess their own land. For these newly-released slaves who had worked non-stop, 24/7, at the whim of their Egyptian masters, God's command to take a day of rest was radical. The Sabbath commandment is framed differently in Exodus and Deuteronomy. We see echoes of the Lord's rest in creation (Exod. 20:11), as well as the emphasis on commanding rescued slaves to rest for a full 24-hour period per week (Deut. 5:15).

Centuries later additional, restrictive pharisaic Sabbath laws had been imposed on the people, which Jesus frequently broke. His deliverance and healing often took place in Sabbath synagogue meetings, enraging the pious Jewish leaders. Jesus told them: 'The Sabbath was made for man, not man for the Sabbath. So the Son of Man is Lord even of the Sabbath' (Mark 2:27–28). God's desire to heal, save and bless His people was not limited to six days a week.

How do you understand Jesus' words: 'The Sabbath was made for man...'? Do you hear this as an expression of God's loving heart towards you? John Mark Comer makes this observation: 'the Sabbath isn't just a twenty-four-hour time slot in your weekly schedule; it's a *spirit* of restfulness that goes with you throughout your week. A way of living with "ease, gratitude, appreciation, peace and prayer". A way of working from rest, not for rest, with nothing to prove.'

In our quest this month to live from a place of rest in God, let's rediscover the holy blessings of Sabbath.

*John Mark Comer, *The Ruthless Elimination of Hurry* (London: Hodder & Stoughton, 2019) p172.

Exodus 20:1–3,8–11; Deuteronomy 5:6–7,12–15

'Remember the Sabbath day by keeping it holy.' (Exod. 20:8)

For prayer and reflection

Heavenly Father, show me how this practice of Sabbath can be relevant for me, then please help me to make practical changes to live it out and enjoy it fully. Amen.

The power **of the Sabbath**

Matthew 6:19–33

'No one can serve two masters… You cannot serve both God and Money.' (v24)

T oday, our key verse closely echoes the first commandment we read yesterday: 'I am the LORD your God… You shall have no other gods before me' (Exod. 20:2–3).

In an article written last year*, the theologian Walter Brueggemann discusses two aspects of time. The first, which he terms 'Promethean' time, is intimately linked to the achievement, success and productivity of our society; and the fact that humans have become 'doings' rather than 'beings'. The other is 'Covenantal' time. Here, free from the pressures of performance and production, we enjoy peace to focus on relationship with our Lord and our neighbours. Central to this is Sabbath rest, as we pause to worship God, reflect on creation and enjoy relationship. 'Sabbath is not simply the pause that refreshes. It is the pause that transforms.'**

At a conference entitled 'The Power of the Sabbath', Gary Grant, founder of The Entertainer toy shop, spoke of his decision in 1994 (as UK Sunday Trading laws were relaxed) to keep his stores closed on Sundays. By 2000, landlords of large shopping centres were refusing him premises. Five years later, when six of his competitors (with 150 stores) had ceased trading, landlords began offering premises to him for use six days a week. The Lord had honoured his decision to put Sabbath-keeping before profit margins, blessing his business.

In Exodus 16, we read that while the Israelites were in the wilderness, the Lord provided double portions of manna on the day before the Sabbath so that the people would rest. How do today's readings challenge you?

For prayer and reflection

Lord, show me if I am putting money, or any other idol, before You. I want to serve You wholeheartedly and enjoy Your Sabbath rest. Amen.

*Walter Brueggemann, *Quarantine Fatigue or Sabbath Rest: A Reflection on Psalm 31*, published online in Church Anew, 7 May 2020.

**Brueggemann, *Sabbath as Resistance: Saying No to the Culture of Now* with Study Guide (Louisville, KY: Westminster John Knox Press, 2017) p45.

The wonder of **sleep**

Psalm 3:5; 4:8;
1 Kings 19:1–8

'I lie down and sleep; I wake again, because the LORD sustains me.'
(Psa. 3:5)

The Greek view that a person is divided into body and soul has influenced Christianity for centuries. A subtle implication can be that 'spiritual' things are godlier than anything related to our body. Jesus did not think this way. The Hebrews viewed us as embodied spiritual beings; whole, not fragmented, people. Feasting and expressing intimate, marital love were part of their Sabbath celebration. Everything about us is important, interconnected and holy.

In studying rest, I discovered that sleep is perhaps the most undervalued yet extraordinary healing, enriching and creative gift of God – and we need it! Our body is repaired; immune system strengthened to detect attack; emotional health recalibrated; motor skills sharpened to learn movements we cannot master without sleep; short-term memory bank emptied into long-term storage, ready for future information; cognitive function improved; grief soothed by dreams; creativity exponentially increased, as disparate ideas interconnect. The list is endless. If you, like me, have burnt the candle at both ends to *do* more for the Lord while awake, please read the life-changing book *Why We Sleep*.

Today, we read of Elijah sleeping, being fed by an angel, nourished and restored after the emotional and spiritual expenditure of his contest at Mount Carmel. God cared for his physical needs. After exhausting months of helping to nurse my mother with terminal cancer, I spent three days on retreat at a peaceful, Spirit-filled convent. Unexpectedly, I found myself sleeping much of the time. The Lord knew what I too most needed: food, rest – and sleep.

*In Matthew Walker's, *Why We Sleep* (London: Allen Lane, 2017) help is also offered to those suffering with poor sleep, and insight given into sleep disorders.

For prayer and reflection

Lord, thank You for the miraculous working of my mind and body. Help me to reassess, with You, how I look after them – and to prioritise Your amazing gift of sleep. Amen.

Invited by Jesus

....

Matthew 11:28–30

'Come to me, all you who are weary and burdened, and I will give you rest.'

Each weekend, we'll be reflecting on these life-giving verses from Matthew's Gospel: 'Come to me…' Jesus invites those who are weary from carrying too much, who are 'tired… Worn out… Burned out on religion' (*The Message*). What do we do when we feel like this? Are we tempted to switch off from God and switch on the TV? When overwhelmed, do we turn to friends for help but forget our Lord? Sometimes, turning to Him seems the hardest thing to do.

I used to read Jesus' words, 'Come to me', as a command but they are, in fact, an invitation. Jesus knows that we can have a tendency to be independent and self-sufficient, refusing to acknowledge our exhaustion. But He never forces His help on us.

The word 'Come' implies movement and choice. This weekend, how could you offer your weariness to Jesus and allow Him to bring you rest? He promises you: 'I will give you rest' – not 'I might be able to help' or 'I'll do my best'. If we come, He will help. He is interceding for us. He is on our side and will always be with us. He is trustworthy and faithful.

Hear Jesus' invitation to you now: 'Come to me'.

....

Optional further reading

Isaiah 40:25–31

John Mark Comer, *The Ruthless Elimination of Hurry*

Helping you
and helping others

Mental health is one of the big topics right now and it's extremely important to God. Whether you are struggling, or you're supporting someone else, we've got a range of resources that will help you.

Our Insight range includes books, devotionals and online courses. We are passionate about people's wellbeing, and so we cover topics that many people struggle with but that are often overlooked, feared or misunderstood. We look at real-life examples, theory and biblical wisdom, so that you can take steps forward.

Visit: **waverleyabbeyresources.org/insight**

Seated in heavenly places

**Ephesians
1:15–2:10**

'And God raised us up with Christ and seated us with him in the heavenly realms in Christ Jesus' (2:6)

Today's key verse both challenges and inspires me: I have died with Christ, been raised with Christ and am now 'seated ... with [God] in the heavenly realms in Christ Jesus'. In his book *Sit, Walk, Stand*, Watchman Nee explains that the extent to which we grasp this incredible spiritual truth will affect our daily Christian life – and in whose strength, anointing and authority we live. As we understand our position with Christ, we have His power to walk out our life – and to stand against Satan's temptations and attacks. Paul, the writer of Ephesians, had learned to live from this place of authority with Jesus and under the anointing of the Holy Spirit, 'his incomparably great power for us who believe' (Eph. 1:19).

Jesus had promised His disciples that after His ascension to heaven He would send the Holy Spirit to fill and empower them to live an emboldened, fruitful life. We marvel at the transformation of His disciples on the day of Pentecost when the Holy Spirit comes upon them (Acts 1:1–9; 2:1–47). Filled with God's love and compassion, they witness boldly, command healing and share their possessions. Their communities are transformed.

We too can receive God's Holy Spirit. Our ascended Lord has done everything for us to be filled daily with His Spirit; to live and work from His Sabbath rest. We have nothing to prove or earn. By living in His grace and His empowering, we will bear spiritual fruit. 'For we are God's handiwork, created in Christ Jesus to do good works, which God prepared in advance for us to do' (Eph. 2:10). God will work through you.

**For prayer
and reflection**

Lord Jesus Christ, fill me again today with Your Holy Spirit and open my eyes to the reality of this wonderful truth: I am seated with You in the heavenly realms. Amen.

Shining **as lights**

Many years ago, I served in a Christian ministry based in a château in Northern France. Still recovering from burnout, with limited energy for physical, practical work, I enthusiastically participated in the worship and prayer. Our team workload was huge, as we frequently hosted visiting groups. Feeling guilty for not responding to the visible, practical needs, I asked, 'Lord, how do I cope with all this busyness – and who can I serve?' Immediately, I pictured a candle and felt Him suggesting that I was the candle shining His light. The more busily I rushed about, the more the flame flickered and dimmed. The more I rested in His presence, the brighter the flame shone. I sensed the Lord telling me that as I rested, my light shining, He would draw people to me. And so it proved. One by one, visitors would seek me out for prayer and encouragement.

How easy it is when we're healthy and well to rush about, our candle flame flickering to near extinction – not realising that, in stillness and rest in God, the light of His presence will shine ever more brightly.

Sue, a fellow trainee, woke very early each morning to spend an hour in worship and prayer. On her return to our dorm, her face shone radiantly. Likewise, we read of the radiant face of Moses on his return from encounters with God.

Jesus, 'the light of the world', calls us to be light in our world, both by acts of compassion, love and service, and by reflecting His 'light of life' within us (John 8:12). How can you enjoy the Lord's presence today and allow the Holy Spirit within you to burn more brightly?

Exodus 34:1–3,28–35; Matthew 5:14–16

'let your light shine before others, that they may… glorify your Father in heaven.' (Matt. 5:16)

For prayer and reflection

Heavenly Father, help me to recentre my thoughts, senses and emotions, and to be still. Fill me again with the love and light of Your Holy Spirit, I pray. Amen.

In the **presence** of the Lord

**Psalm 84:1–12;
27:4–5**

'Blessed are those
who dwell in your
house... Better is
one day in your
courts than a
thousand
elsewhere'
(84:4,10)

An abiding springtime memory was watching an adult blue tit feed its baby fledgling, only two metres from where my husband and I were sitting. It was a rare privilege for wild birds to choose to be in our presence, trusting us and caring for their young. I recalled this wonderfully evocative psalm of the Sons of Korah, Levites 'in charge of the work of the service' of the house of God (1 Chron. 9:19, ESV). We read of sparrows and swallows finding a place to nest near the altar; as the psalmists describe, being in God's presence within the Temple brings joy, blessing, peace and safety for human, beast and bird alike.

In Psalm 27, David shares his passionate longing to dwell in the beauty and protection of the Lord's presence. Another tender image of the place of safety and rest in God is found in the blessing to Benjamin: 'Let the beloved of the LORD rest secure in him, for he shields him all day long, and the one the LORD loves rests between his shoulders' (Deut. 33:12). I visualise a child carried on their father's back; or a shepherd, gently bringing home a lamb or injured sheep.

All these images cause me to ponder: 'Where is the place of rest?' Surely, it is in the presence of our Lord, whatever our circumstances. A persecuted Chinese Christian leader, imprisoned for years, was condemned to work daily in a cesspool. When asked how he endured such horrific, insanitary conditions, he would smile and say that the presence of the Lord was so strongly with him, he saw it as his rose garden. Being alone with His Lord in worship, peace and rest was a blessing – even in a cesspool.

**For prayer
and reflection**

How can you
become more
aware of the Lord's
presence with
you today?

Absolute trust in God's **care**

L et's meditate today on this beautiful psalm. David likens himself to a weaned child with its mother – a child who, having been fed, is content to fall asleep on his mother. In healthy parent-child relationships, children do not question that their parents will provide for them, will be there when they fall and comfort them when they cry. This is the bond of attachment and trust the Lord wants us, His beloved children, to have with Him. David shows absolute trust in his heavenly Father's ability to handle situations too big for him; he humbly commits himself to God's care.

'But I have calmed and quietened myself, I am like a weaned child with its mother; like a weaned child I am content.' (v2)

Centuries later, as He begins His ministry, Jesus hears His Father's voice: 'This is my Son, whom I love; with him I am well pleased' (Matt. 3:17). Following this astounding affirmation of His Father's love and His own identity, Jesus has a foundational security in who He is. It anchors Him, despite false accusations and relentless scorn from religious leaders, and even during His agony in Gethsemane. Our security and rest is likewise founded on our knowledge of God's forgiveness, His total acceptance and His ceaseless love for us, whatever happens.

Jesus teaches us to have childlike faith. Can we trust our Father God and nestle into Him as a child to its mother's breast? This intimate image draws and challenges me. Today, I choose to lay down questions about my future, my concerns for the wellbeing of those I love, and to trust in the unfailing love and daily provision of my heavenly Father, who promises to feed me and supply all my needs as I walk with Him.

For prayer and reflection

Abba, Father, thank You that I am Your child and You love me. Deepen my relationship with You, so that I can learn to trust You more completely. Amen.

Rest for the **battle weary**

Psalm 23:1–6; 62:1–8

'He makes me lie down in green pastures… leads me beside quiet waters… refreshes my soul.' (23:2–3)

Waverley Abbey House, home to Waverley Abbey Resources, is a beautiful mansion set in extensive grounds beside a small lake and water meadow. To sit beside the lake, overlooking the ruins of a medieval Cistercian abbey (a house of prayer for centuries), is a wonderful experience of retreat and reflection; a perfect match for the psalmist's words.

The Lord called me to work for Waverley Abbey Resources (CWR then) as an editor following a time of intense, costly spiritual battle. I use these words advisedly: as a leader of a Christian organisation, I had seen colleagues involved in witchcraft transferred into my co-leader's work team; while groundless, false and serious allegations had been made against me by a co-worker's wife, her irrational accusations and threatening behaviour flaring up every prayer week. The Lord knew how spiritually and emotionally exhausted I was, drawing me aside to Waverley to spend hours reading His Word as part of my work, and to walk, sit and pray by the lake at lunchtime.

King David, who penned today's psalms 3,000 years ago, knew what it was to face spiritual and physical exhaustion, to be battle weary – and to find rest, refreshment and new strength in God. Listen again to his words: 'Truly my soul finds rest in God; my salvation comes from him. Truly he is my rock and my salvation; he is my fortress, I shall never be shaken. How long will you assault me?… they take delight in lies… Yes, my soul, find rest in God; my hope comes from him' (Psa. 62:1–5).

In which areas of life are you battle weary, needing restoration? The Lord seeks to draw you apart, for you to rest, be healed and refreshed. Come to Him.

For prayer and reflection

Lord, show me today where and how I can rest in You. Renew my strength, hope and trust in You; restore my soul, I pray. Amen.

Become part of someone's testimony

Our Bible reading notes are read by hundreds of thousands of people around the world, and *Inspiring Women Every Day* and *Every Day with Jesus* have recently been made free in the UK. We want everyone, whatever their financial means, to have access to these resources that help them walk each day with our Saviour.

Here's what one *Inspiring Women Every Day* reader wrote to us:

I just wanted to send a message to say how much I've appreciated the most recent readings in IWED. They have been insightful, honest and have deeply touched my needs through the work of the Holy Spirit I know.

As we trust in God's provision, we know there are costs to providing this ministry. Do you have a passion for God's Word changing lives? Could supporting this vision be a way in which you serve?

A gift of just £2 a month from you will put daily Bible reading notes into the hands of at least one person who is hungry to know God and experience His presence every day.

Visit **waverleyabbeyresources.org/donate** to become part of someone's testimony, or use the form at the back of these notes.

Weekend

What are you carrying?

....

Matthew 11:28–30

'Come to me, all you who are weary and burdened, and I will give you rest.' (v28)

Rhossili in Wales is a special meeting place with the Lord for me. On my last visit, as I left the clifftop car park heading for the long, descending steps to the breath-taking beach, I felt an urgent whisper: 'You're carrying too much and must halve your load. If not, you'll regret it on the way back up…' While discarding unnecessary items, I sensed the Lord speak again: 'The same is true in life. You are carrying too much. To accomplish My future plans for you, you must learn to let go of half your load.' Sobering words. It has not been easy. I want to be more free to travel, to be involved overseas. Yet I still need to let go of spiritual burdens no longer mine to carry and to live more simply.

Jesus states: 'I am the vine; you are the branches'. He then tells us that Father God, the gardener, prunes the healthy growth of the branches, so that we will be even more fruitful (John 15:1–8). Which shoots, branches or even dead wood is God wanting to cut away from your life? Will you allow Him to prune you, for His glory? Can you yield to His words, trust Him and allow Him to lighten Your load?

....

Optional further reading
John 14:15–15:17

Hurry sickness

Our rest in Christ is constantly under attack. This week, we'll consider a few enemies of rest, starting with a contemporary malaise termed 'hurry sickness'. Fascinatingly, 3,000 years ago King David described his contemporaries who 'rush about, heaping up wealth'. Hurry and rush are not modern phenomena, but signs of a deeper human condition.

My husband and I love choosing holiday destinations where the pace of life is slower. Once there, we feel that we can breathe; priorities come into sharper focus; decisions become easier to make. So why, on our return home, do we allow our lives to speed up again?

You will probably have experienced lockdown last year. In the UK, roads were quiet, almost empty; shopping centres deserted. A section of the population slowed down and found unexpected space in their busy schedules. While writing and working part-time for a school, I joined a daily prayer community, which has deepened my spiritual life. The simplicity of my home routine left me feeling more grounded; rooted, like the tree described in Psalm 1. I discovered the beauty of wild purple orchids 15 minutes' walk away. As Claudia Hammond comments: 'the act of walking appears to stretch and deepen time. This is why we find walking so restful. So much of life these days is speeded up. Walking slows us down.'*

I reconnected with my neighbours. I gained much. What about you? Are you still enjoying Sabbath moments, pauses to take a walk or to greet passers-by? What did the Lord teach you in that unusual time? Has your pace of life now sped up again? If so, what steps could you take to slow down?

*Claudia Hammond, *The Art of Rest: How to Find Respite in the Modern Age* (Edinburgh: Canongate Books Ltd., 2019) p96.

Psalm 1:1–3; 39:1–7

'Surely everyone goes around like a mere phantom; in vain they rush about, heaping up wealth without knowing whose it will finally be.' (39:6)

For prayer and reflection

Meditate today on the first three verses of Psalm 1, and on Jesus' words: 'Abide in me, and I in you' (John 15:4, ESV). What do these words mean for you?

Anxiety

Isaiah 26:1–4;
John 14:15–27

'You will keep in
perfect peace those
whose minds are
steadfast, because
they trust in you.'
(Isa. 26:3)

I t was 2am on a September night. Never had I been so anxious. Although well prepared, I was terrified at the prospect of starting my first teaching role. Over and over, I listened to these words: 'Thou dost keep him in perfect peace, whose mind is stayed on Thee, because he trusts in Thee'. The truth gradually calming my soul, I finally found rest. Those early days were not easy, but I learned to trust God.

I've discovered that trust can be spelt out:

T – Tell the Lord all your worries. Speak them out, write them down. Fear lingering unexposed will grow. Peter exhorts us: 'Cast all your anxiety on him because he cares for you' (1 Pet. 5:7).

R – Release your anxieties into the Lord's hands. Physically, you could gather small stones and name each of your concerns, as you place the stones individually at the foot of a cross, a lit candle or an object symbolising the Lord.

U – Understand the immensity of the Lord's love for you: 'For as high as the heavens are above the earth, so great is his love for those who fear him' (Psa. 103:11). Focus on how much more powerful the Lord is than anything you are facing.

S – Submit yourself and the outcome to the Lord. Daniel's friends, when faced with a fiery furnace for refusing to bow to an image, declared their trust in the Lord whatever the outcome (Dan. 3). (This is enormous, I know.)

T – Turn your eyes upon Jesus; fix your mind on Him and hear His words: 'my peace I give you... Do not let your hearts be troubled and do not be afraid (John 14:27). 'I am with you always, to the very end of the age' (Matt. 28:20).

**For prayer
and reflection**

**Lord, help me to
lay my worries and
concerns at Your
feet. May I see how
truly loving,
compassionate
and powerful You
are. I choose to
trust You. Amen.**

*From *Thou dost keep him in perfect peace* by Robert Stoodley © Copyright 1978 Sovereign Music UK. Used by permission.

The danger of **distraction**

D id you know that algorithms are built into social media sites to capture as much of your time as possible? This means that interesting items will pop up to subtly distract you away from your original purpose. A deliberate ploy, this is partly why social media can become so addictive.

Today we read of Martha being worried and distracted by all the preparations. We can only imagine Jesus' words to us now, when our potential for distraction has multiplied. How difficult it is to switch off from everything and sit, as Mary does, at Jesus' feet to pray, worship or meditate on Scripture, without being side-tracked by to-do lists, messages, emails, reminders and other competing demands...

Like Martha, I can be drawn away from what is most essential. In the Parable of the Sower, seed which had grown into a healthy plant was finally choked by the thorns surrounding it, thus preventing it from bearing mature fruit. Jesus describes those thorns as 'life's worries, riches and pleasures' (Luke 8:14), which prevent the disciple from maturing to their full potential and bearing the fruit God intends. Sadly, at times I've seen myself in this very parable.

So could you reflect today on what distracts you – and how you could avoid it? Identify one area in which you can make a change. Then, when you've seen success, reward yourself and move on to the next. Start small: for example, perhaps you could limit checking messages, emails or social media to certain times each day? Don't overwhelm yourself by trying to tackle everything at once. The Lord is our helper, and with His help we can grow and mature, one step at a time.

Luke 8:4–15; 10:38–42

'But Martha was distracted by all the preparations that had to be made.' (10:40)

For prayer and reflection

To meditate on today: 'For where your treasure is, there your heart will be also' (Luke 12:34). 'God is the strength of my heart and my portion for ever' (Psa. 73:26).

Tyranny of the **urgent**

Mark 1:32–38;
Luke 8:41–55

"'Who touched me?' Jesus asked.'
(Luke 8:45)

H ave you experienced stressful times of frantic activity in which rest becomes a distant memory? I certainly have.

Today, we see Jesus at the end of a full day, surrounded by crowds seeking healing. He sets off very early the next morning 'to a solitary place' to pray. As He'll later tell His critics, Jesus wants His priorities to be those of His Father; He will do only what He sees His Father doing. After spending time in His Father's presence, He then makes a surprising decision. He plans to leave the town, in which there was so much fruit for the kingdom the day before, to visit another village where an unknown reception awaits Him. His disciples don't understand: You're needed! 'Everyone is looking for you!' But Jesus knows the importance of His message being preached more widely: 'That is why I have come' (Mark 1:37–38).

In Luke's Gospel, we find Jesus again being called for urgently, this time to heal Jairus' dying daughter. He agrees to go. Halted in His tracks by the touch of a desperate woman, whose 12 years of constant bleeding drive her to flout the Jewish laws, this time Jesus knows how important it is to stop – and her bold faith results in healing and blessing.

In daily life, tasks fall into four categories: non-urgent and unimportant, urgent and unimportant, non-urgent and important, urgent and important. How often do urgent, unimportant tasks take up our day, while important yet non-urgent, God-given tasks remain undone for months on end? When this happens, we sense an inner unease: life is passing by, yet we are missing out on what is important, our calling.

For prayer and reflection

Lord, it's hard to know what's important when urgent demands are being made of me. Please help me to prioritise what's most essential. Amen.

Superwoman syndrome

ears ago, I participated in a Bible study course entitled *Excelling as a Woman*, based on this Hebrew wisdom poem on the 'ideal' woman. However, this woman is a composite of the virtues women possess, as no *one* person could live life on all the levels she did – at least, not if she were to stay physically and emotionally healthy! This woman was not only up early before dawn, but her lamp was still burning late at night. Unfortunately, many of us today *do* try to live like her, as I did for years. Not only burning the candle at both ends, but being a perfectionist, if tasks were not completed perfectly I was not satisfied; and whilst there was work still to do I could not rest. Do you recognise that miserable trap?

In his insightful book *The Ruthless Elimination of Hurry*, John Mark Comer makes a crucial point. Not only do we each possess huge potential, but we each have limitations. Created in the image of God, we are made from 'dust' – and are therefore finite not infinite. Comer concisely spells out what limitation means for each of us: 'You. Can't. Do. It. All.'

Yesterday, we read that Jesus was asked to do more than God had assigned Him to do. He refused. People were still hunting Him out to see further miracles and healings, yet He steadfastly insisted that He move on, being guided by His sense of purpose and call from Father God.

Knowing what we are called to do, and therefore by definition realising that we cannot do everything else, is liberating and brings peace. Moreover, saying no to what we are *not* called to leaves space available for the person who is called to do it.

*John Mark Comer, *The Ruthless Elimination of Hurry* (London: Hodder & Stoughton, 2019) p65.

Proverbs 31:10–30

'Charm is deceptive, and beauty is fleeting; but a woman who fears the LORD is to be praised.' (v30)

For prayer and reflection

Lord, thank You that You have created me with limitations. May I accept and embrace them – to devote myself more fully to the work You have planned for me. Amen.

The humble King

....

Matthew 11:28–30

'learn from me, for I am gentle and humble in heart' (v29)

Jesus is a gentle man. Not only that, He is compassionate, forgiving, gracious and full of the Holy Spirit's fruit (love, joy, peace, forbearance, kindness, goodness, faithfulness and self-control; Gal. 5:22–23). Neither chauvinistic nor condescending, Jesus honoured and respected women, treating them as individuals with the right to be His disciples – in a culture which reserved this right for men alone. In his beautiful song *Humble King*, Brenton Brown describes this Jesus, who loves the meek and poor in spirit, heals the grieving and broken-hearted, and washes His disciples' feet.

How well do we know this Jesus? Is our view of Him distorted, perhaps due to our upbringing or previous experiences of men? Might we need to view our Saviour through a new lens?

This weekend I invite you to try something different: to write a prayer, poem or letter to this Jesus, the gentle man. Try to fully express your feelings, interests and concerns to Him. He is the *friend* of sinners, the good shepherd of His sheep. He is 'gentle and humble in heart', and He loves you.

....

Optional further reading

John 8:2–11; 13:1–17

Philippians 2:1–11

Peace in the storm

Today, we find the disciples with Jesus, sailing across the Sea of Galilee, when a huge, unexpected storm blows up. Yet Jesus, who has fallen asleep, remains soundly sleeping as the situation, in the disciples' eyes, grows ever more critical. In sheer terror they awaken Him, begging Him to act before they all die. His response is remarkable. Rather than empathising and calming their nerves, He commands the wind and the waves to die down, then questions the disciples about their lack of faith.

In recent times, our world has faced the unpredictable, turbulent, life-threatening storm of Covid-19. How can this story help us? Firstly, Jesus offers us His incredible inner peace, just as He gave His disciples: 'My peace I give you, my peace I leave with you. I do not give as the world gives. Do not let your hearts be troubled and do not be afraid' (John 14:27). However fearful our circumstances, His peace can hold us.

Secondly, Jesus commands us not to be afraid. This means we have a choice: whether or not to give in to our natural fear of the circumstances. It is hard not to, but the Spirit will help us as we resolve to not allow anxious thoughts to dominate our mind.

Thirdly, His disciples were rebuked for their lack of faith – for believing that Jesus would abandon them to die. Storm or not, Jesus is *always* with us. He wants us to trust in His love and goodness rather than give in to whatever fear we have. Knowing that we're held in the loving arms of Jesus, who desires to fill us with His peace, will help us to navigate even the most turbulent waters of life.

Mark 4:35–41;
John 14:27

'Peace I leave with you; my peace I give you… do not be afraid.'
(John 14:27)

For prayer and reflection

Heavenly Father, when circumstances threaten to overwhelm me, please fill me with the peace Jesus promises and deepen my trust in Your love and goodness. Amen.

The disciple Jesus **loved**

**1 John 4:7–21;
John 13:21–25**

'And so we know
and rely on the
love God has for
us. God is love.'
(1 John 4:16)

I n his famous painting *Last Supper*, Valentin de
Boulogne wonderfully depicts the closeness that
existed between Jesus and His disciple John. The
artist represents John leaning against Jesus' chest while
reclining at the table to eat. This was the moment when,
in a whisper, John enquired who the betrayer would be.

When appointing them as His disciples, Jesus had
nicknamed John and his brother James 'sons of thunder',
due to their fiery temper. Years later, this same John
became known as 'the apostle of love'. As an elderly
father figure of the Church, John wrote letters from
exile on the Isle of Patmos, repeatedly emphasising the
importance of love and unity (1 John 4:7–21).

Had John learned what it was to rest in God, just as
he physically rested on his master's chest at the Last
Supper? What was the secret of his growth in maturity,
leading to a changed personality? The answer, I believe,
is found in the words John uses to describe himself: 'the
disciple whom Jesus loved' (John 13:23). Knowing that
he was loved by God had shaped his identity.

A close friend once gave me a Bible sticker: 'Know
yourself loved' – a truth that at that time I desperately
needed to take to heart. Do you, like John, know
yourself loved, as you are? Do you know that God likes
you and loves you deeply enough to die for you? Do you
know how valuable you are as a unique member of His
body – however unimportant or useless you might feel
(1 Cor. 12:12–27)?

Say this aloud to yourself now, and repeat it when
necessary: I am a disciple Jesus loves.

**For prayer
and reflection**

**Lord, You tell me
that I am of
immense value
and I am deeply
loved. Please
make that real to
me, so that I see
myself as You see
me. Amen.**

The joy of **solitude**

Luke 1:5–25

'Elizabeth became pregnant and for five months remained in seclusion. "The Lord has done this for me"' (vv24–25)

We're not told much about Elizabeth, a biblical heroine of mine. We do know that she was a godly woman, the daughter of a priest, and was unable to bear children. In a culture where child-bearing was seen as a woman's primary role, and infertility a curse, she must have suffered terribly.

However, Elizabeth remains faithful to God. Then, one astonishing day, Zechariah arrives home speechless but full of news! An angel has declared that they will bear a child, John – an extraordinary messenger for the Messiah. Now beyond typical child-bearing age, Elizabeth prepares for this unimaginable life change by spending months 'in seclusion'. What does she do? Perhaps she takes encouragement from the lives of Sarah, Rebekah, Hannah – each mother to a Jewish leader, following painful years of infertility; maybe she expresses her joy and anxiety about imminent motherhood to God, and rests during her early pregnancy, emotionally processing the change to come. When Mary meets her (Luke 1:41), she is at peace. What can we learn from her?

In my own life, when facing significant challenges or changes (the call to overseas mission, forthcoming marriage, my mother's unexpected death), I've also found it vital to spend time apart with the Lord. In a place of retreat, I've rested, pouring out my questions and emotions to God, receiving peace, clarity, renewed trust and, on one occasion, hours of much-needed sleep.

Are you facing a major challenge or change? Could you follow Elizabeth's example? How might you practise the spiritual discipline of solitude, to focus on and rest in the Lord?

For prayer and reflection

Lord, teach me to value quietness and solitude, as Elizabeth did, in order to draw on Your strength, receive Your love and wisdom, and deepen my closeness with You. Amen.

Jill Weber

Jill Weber serves on the International Leadership Team of 24-7 Prayer, and is the Global Convenor of the Order of the Mustard Seed, a religious order within 24-7 Prayer. This is how it all began...

It was the year 2000. I had been training for six years as a local church planter, on a path towards ordination. Invited to a prayer meeting, I naively walked in, completely unaware that on that evening the trajectory of my life would completely change. When we pray 'Your kingdom come', we are invoking the person and the purposes of God, giving Him permission to come and be who He is in our midst, and to do those things that only He can do. Pray at your own risk. Anything can happen.

The meeting was led by a team from a House of Prayer – a community dedicated to praying for their region, nation and world. That night, those leading combined worship and prayer

in ways that were unfamiliar to me but opened a wide doorway to God's presence. I'm a worship leader, and had never really seen myself as a 'prayer person', but fusing worship and prayer together made my heart come alive in unexpected ways. I knew this was something that I was created to do.

Invited by the Lord, I set aside my long-held dream of church planting and began to explore the completely unfamiliar terrain of beginning (and becoming) a House of Prayer – whatever that was!

Over the next 17 years I gathered other pilgrims and practitioners. We explored how we could shape our lifestyles around prayer, mission and justice, joined by local churches. What might happen if we embedded a community of prayer in an impoverished city area? If we created an interdenominational prayer room in a social enterprise cafe in the red light district? If we offered community dinners to neighbours and strangers? We even rented a lorry, kitted it out as a 'pop up' prayer room in the middle of our city, and offered prayer and water to passers-by!

'You're a prayer missionary – your job is to pray?' People asked. 'Isn't that boring?'

'Ha!' I responded. 'When you create space and invite God to come and fill it however He wishes, boring isn't on the menu. Anything can happen!'

Fast forward to 2016. I went to another prayer meeting. You would think that I would know better by now, and have the sense to stay away. Prayer meetings are dangerous. Anything can happen.

Once more, I was interrupted. Invited by God to relocate from our native Canada to the UK. I joined the 24-7 Prayer leadership and began to develop what we now call the Seed Community. 24-7 Prayer is a global movement that exists to revive the church and to rewire culture. We create prayer resources, catalyse prayer initiatives, and sometimes we plant prayer communities.

Waverley Abbey House has kindly made space for the Seed Community. Our residential House of Prayer community will cultivate prayer onsite and online. We've created the Waverley Abbey Prayer Room in the house, open to the public so that anyone can come and join in. Through online and onsite short courses and retreats, we invite others to explore and experiment with various aspects of spiritual formation and spiritual disciplines.

The original Waverley Abbey was the first Cistercian Monastery in the UK, established in 1128. We know that even in the 700s the land was used by a praying community. There have been people praying here for over a thousand years! Waverley Abbey itself planted another 11 prayer communities across the UK. What might happen if we pick up where they left off? What might God do? Anything can happen.

You can read more of Jill's story in her book, *Even the Sparrow*. Also visit **jillweber.com** and **24-7prayer.com**

The comfort of **companionship**

Luke 1:26–45,56

'Elizabeth… exclaimed: "Blessed are you among women, and blessed is the child you will bear!"' (vv41–42)

Today the Church celebrates Annunciation Day, when the Angel Gabriel brought God's world-changing message to Mary, a devout Jewish teenager in Nazareth. After Mary has recovered from the initial shock of the news, plus the excitement that the Lord has chosen *her* to bear His Son, what thoughts run through her mind? Will Joseph and her family believe her story? (In her culture, adultery was punished by stoning.) But Gabriel has offered a lifeline, telling Mary that her relative Elizabeth is pregnant, despite having passed typical child-bearing age. So Mary travels miles to spend time with Elizabeth, perhaps hoping that she can offer godly support for her own situation.

Seeking out the prayerful counsel, support and companionship of faith-filled friends can be vital when we're facing turbulent times. Jesus Himself, during His agony in Gethsemane, entreated His three closest friends, Peter, James and John, to draw near to Him and pray (Matt. 26:36–39). The intercessions and wisdom of someone who has experienced what we're going through, whose testimony can encourage our faith and who is committed to being there for us, all are invaluable in helping us find God's peace and rest.

For prayer and reflection

Take a moment to thank the Lord for your friends. Could you encourage one today? Or, if you are struggling or feel alone, could you turn to a friend for support?

Can you, like Elizabeth, offer spiritual support to a friend whose world has been turned upside down? On hearing Elizabeth's Holy Spirit-inspired greeting, Mary's heart is filled with praise; her faith strengthened. She declares her confidence and joy in a profoundly inspiring song (vv46–55); and doubtless returns home, after John's birth, in a place of deeper faith and peace.

The secret of **contentment**

How can we be at peace, praising God, when our world is in utter chaos? Today, we see Paul and Silas flogged then thrown into jail in Philippi. Their response? To pray and sing joyful praise to God at midnight.

Paul knows a secret: how to rest in his Lord, whatever his circumstances. In his letters, he describes his sufferings: beatings, imprisonment, floggings, shipwrecks, near starvation (2 Cor. 11:23–31); he'd also known times of plenty, fellowship and celebration. Through it all, he says, 'I have learned the secret of being content in any and every situation... I can do all this through him who gives me strength' (Phil. 4:12–13). He submits his future into God's hands, trusting in this truth: 'in all things God works for the good of those who love him... I am convinced that neither death nor life... nor anything else in all creation, will be able to separate us from the love of God that is in Christ Jesus our Lord' (Rom. 8:28,38–39).

Praise releases God's powerful presence into our situation. In suffering, it's countercultural and counterintuitive – society often encourages us to grumble in our troubles. I admit that I can struggle to praise in this way but, when I do, my spirit is lifted and I experience new peace. The result of praise in Philippi? Prison doors flung open and the jailer's family, having witnessed the outstanding faith and compassion of Paul and Silas, turned to Christ.

Are you facing circumstances in which you could choose to pray and worship, rather than descend into despair? Be encouraged: the Lord is with you to bring His peace and joy into your situation.

Acts 16: 16–19,22–33; Philippians 4:4–7,11–13

'I have learned the secret of being content in... every situation... whether living in plenty or in want.' (Phil. 4:12)

For prayer and reflection

Lord, You know how much I struggle in difficult circumstances. Help me to trust in Your goodness and love, so that I can worship You and experience Your peace. Amen.

Living lightly the 'Jesus way'

....

Matthew 11:28–30

'Take my yoke upon you and learn from me… For my yoke is easy and my burden is light' (vv29–30)

As we conclude our reflections on these profound words of Jesus, we'll consider the imagery He employs. Oxen were often seen yoked together to plough a field. Is Jesus saying that we should be linked to Him, side by side, as we do life together? Yes, but much more. In His day, rabbinic teachers spoke of their 'yoke' to encompass the breadth of their teaching; their approach to life. Jesus, a rabbi, was therefore saying, 'Live my way and follow my teaching'. Paraphrased wonderfully in *The Message*, this reads: 'Walk with me and work with me—watch how I do it. Learn the unforced rhythms of grace… Keep company with me and you'll learn to live freely and lightly' (vv29–30).

What do I need to give up, simplify or adapt to live 'freely and lightly'? I invite you to join me in this challenging prayer:

'Jesus, I am guilty of filling my life to the brim and squeezing out many opportunities to rest with You. My burdens and tiredness are often self-inflicted. I surrender to You my diary, my to-do list, my obligations and ambitions, and I ask You to teach me to live and learn at Your pace. Amen.'*

*Prayer of Yielding by Carla Harding taken from Lectio 365 App, February 3, 2020, © 24-7 Prayer

....

Optional further reading

Galatians 1:1–6:18.
David Seamands, *Healing Grace: Finding Freedom from the Performance Trap* (Indianapolis, USA: Light and Life Communications, 1999)

It is **well** with my soul

'since we are
surrounded by
such a great cloud
of witnesses… let
us run with
perseverance the
race' (12:1)

The hymn with the greatest power to lift my spirit begins: 'When peace like a river attendeth my way, when sorrows like sea billows roll, whatever my lot, Thou hast taught me to say, It is well, it is well with my soul.' If it's new to you, please listen to it in full, as today we read of its author, Horatio Spafford, one of the 'great cloud of witnesses' gone before us.

In 1871, Horatio and his wife, Annie, lost their only son to scarlet fever, then most of their life savings, invested in Chicago property destroyed by fire. In 1873, a family holiday to Europe was planned to join their friend, the evangelist Dwight Moody, on a mission trip. Delayed by last-minute business, Horatio sent his wife and four young daughters on ahead. Tragically, their ship struck another vessel mid-Atlantic, sinking rapidly. A devastating 266 passengers were lost. Ten days later, Horatio received Annie's telegram: 'Saved alone. What do I do?' Heartbroken, Horatio took the next sailing and, midway through the voyage, the captain pinpointed the exact location where the stricken vessel had sunk and Horatio's daughters had perished. It was then Horatio Spafford penned these astonishingly moving words.

Years later, Horatio and Annie, with newly-born children, relocated to Jerusalem, founding a Christian community to serve Muslims, Arabs, Jews and Christians alike. This work continued throughout the First and Second World Wars. Truly, a remarkable story of a family whose personal tragedy and loss were powerfully redeemed by the Lord to bring comfort, strength, encouragement and hope to others.

**For prayer
and reflection**

Father God, may I know Your comfort so that I can comfort others – and be able to declare that, whatever my circumstances, it is well with my soul. Amen.

Resting in His **promises**

Psalm 23:1–6;
John 10:2–15

'The LORD is my
shepherd, I lack
nothing.'
(Psa. 23:1)

I'd like us to spend a second day looking at David's beautiful psalm of trust and dependence on his Lord. This time, we'll reflect on each phrase. To help you still your thoughts and emotions, try to focus on a lit candle or beautiful flower, or imagine calm, peaceful water. Become aware of your breathing: breathe in the Lord's presence ('I receive You, Lord Jesus'), and offer Him your cares as you breathe out ('I give You…').

Dwell on Psalm 23, phrase by phrase, turning the words over in your mind and asking Jesus to speak promises back to you. 'The LORD is my shepherd' (v1). Jesus says, 'I am the good shepherd'. His plans for you are *good* (John 10:11; Jer. 29:11). 'I lack nothing' (v1). As you seek Him and His kingdom purposes, He will supply all your needs (Matt. 6:19–34). 'He makes me lie down in green pastures, he leads me beside quiet waters, he refreshes my soul' (vv2–3). Jesus promises to lead us and that you, His sheep, will know His voice (John 10:3–5). Sheep can be very stubborn though! How is God speaking to you today? His words to me this morning were: 'Speak less and listen more'. Will I heed Him? Sometimes, unwilling to stop, we'll only submit to the gentle voice calling us to rest when exhaustion or illness hit us. Will we give ourselves permission to stop and rest?

Why not continue to sit with the Lord, lifting each phrase to Him; allowing Him to speak His promises into your life? Jesus does not promise to remove us from the troubles and hardships of life, but He does promise to be with us, to give us strength and hope, His constant peace and never-ending love.

**For prayer
and reflection**

**Lord Jesus, how
can I act upon the
words You have
spoken to me
today? Thank You
for Your promise of
rest, as I choose to
live life Your way
(Matt. 11:29).
Amen.**

The ultimate **place of rest**

I n concluding our month's reflections, and in light of the devastating Covid-19 pandemic, I don't want to shy away from mentioning the final place of rest, death itself.

As Christians, we believe that death ushers us into heaven – eternal full communion with our Lord – and each of us will, sooner or later, go to be with Him. The Lord promised His disciples that He has gone ahead to prepare a place for us (John 14:1–4); a place where all wrongs will be righted, all suffering and infirmity healed, all injustice ended – and love alone will reign. We'll enter the place of ultimate rest and rejoicing, worshipping with Moses, Elizabeth and Horatio Spafford, among countless others.

Our Lord longs for everyone to one day be with Him in that place. Even while in agony on the cross, Jesus reassured the repentant robber dying beside him, with the words: 'today you will be with me in paradise' (Luke 23:43). Following His resurrection, He appeared to His own brother James, which presumably led to James becoming a follower of Christ (1 Cor. 15:7). How could you and I reach out now to family and friends, in prayer, righting relationships, offering forgiveness, to ensure that they know our love and forgiveness for them – and discover the eternal love of our Lord?

As we look forward in faith to the heavenly city, which will be our eternal destination, may we spend our days sharing our hope with others: the hope of a heaven with no more fear, illness, shame, mourning, tears or pain. For, as the apostle Paul declared, 'For me, to live is Christ, to die is gain' (Phil. 1:21).

**Revelation 7:17;
21:1–4;
Isaiah 25:8**

'There will be no more death, or mourning or crying or pain, for the old order of things has passed away.' (Rev. 21:4)

**For prayer
and reflection**

Lord, You have been victorious over death . May I know Your promised peace here on earth, and eternal rest and rejoicing in the life to come. Amen.

Shameless

REBECCA BERRY

John 13:1–17

'he poured water into a basin and began to wash his disciples' feet, drying them with the towel that was wrapped round him.' (v5)

Jesus, this Easter and beyond, give me a shameless love for You. Amen.

Perhaps it's not a word you would instinctively associate with Him, but, this Easter, I'd love for us to explore the shamelessness of Jesus. As I started thinking about this, I quickly realised it isn't the easiest idea to pin down. Jesus, it turns out, was pretty shameless in a lot of ways – not only because He was guiltless, but because He absolutely knew the truth about who He was – who He *is*.

We might like to think of Him as a nice man who behaved impeccably, and I definitely don't want to commit heresy here. But Jesus also caused a lot of controversy, and was prepared to upset a fair few religious people (so much so that they killed Him for it) to make the lowest of the low feel loved. He shamelessly crossed social, cultural and religious barriers to get through to people that He is *for* them. Is that something that we imitate today, I wonder?

Not meeting the limited, human expectations of other people seems to be something that Jesus was (and is) in the habit of. On this Maundy Thursday, we read about an unusual display of behaviour of His that would at the time have been considered bizarre at best, offensive at worst: He washed His disciples' feet.

Jesus wasn't an insecure man who needed His ranking as 'Saviour of the World' to be signposted with ego and superiority. Instead He shows humility, service, generosity, kindness… love. Here He stoops – perfectly willingly – to the position of a servant, unafraid to go near what were presumably the dirtiest parts of His friends' bodies, to cleanse them of all their muck and dirt. What do you think He was getting at?

Shameless **love**

**John 19:1–3,
15–18**

'The soldiers
twisted together a
crown of thorns
and put it on his
head… And they
slapped him in the
face.' (vv2–3)

S cripture that describes the brutal execution of
Jesus is never an easy read. The Romans had not
only perfected the art of torture, knowing how
to kill in the slowest and most excruciating ways, they
also knew how to shame and humiliate. What strikes me
about this passage today is the mocking and torment
that Jesus went through, as well as the physical agony.
Nothing about His death seemed dignified or heroic;
it was savage entertainment for the mob. But it *was*
glorious. He took death down by taking death on.

In thinking about Jesus' death, I can't help but be
reminded of His birth. A frightened teenage mother
sheltering in a shabby outbuilding as a last resort,
squatting among animals in the middle of a strange and
bustling city, presumably labouring with the assistance
of a bewildered and inexperienced husband – this was
the arrival of the Messiah. Nothing about His story
unfolded in the way people expected. Jesus seems to
be in the habit of using the most humble, disgraceful and
even offensive circumstances to show His love to the
world. I love that. The world's idea of a shameful birth
and a shameful death – fit for a shameless Saviour.

Shame is so out of place in the kingdom of God
that the Son of God was prepared to die, even in this
horrendous way, to remove it from us forever. So, this
Good Friday, imagine all your shame – the worst thing
you've ever done, your bad decisions, your regrets and
your failures – nailed to the cross, and leave it all there.
Because if Jesus didn't die in order to take it away and
bring you back to the Father, then I don't know why
He did.

**For prayer
and reflection**

Jesus, I can't begin
to imagine what
You went through
for me on the cross.
Help me to accept
Your love, and
allow You to do in
my life what You
died to do. Amen.

For joy

Hebrews 12:2

'For the joy that was set before him he endured the cross, scorning its shame, and sat down at the right hand of the throne of God.' (v2)

We typically spend Good Friday reflecting on the agonies Jesus suffered on our behalf, but our focus now shifts to Easter Sunday, and the joy that follows sorrow. This is how The Passion Translation puts today's reading: 'Because his heart was focused on the joy of knowing that you would be his, he endured the agony of the cross and conquered its humiliation'.

Shame was enemy number one, and Jesus took it on in its fullest and most brutal form. He scorned shame; He conquered humiliation (which I think makes it pretty clear what Jesus thinks of shame and humiliation). That's what He went to war *against*, but what was He fighting *for*? For 'the joy of knowing that you would be his'. Knowing you is His joy! He is totally focused on making you His.

Not only did Jesus put shame in its place on the cross, but a lot of His ministry was focused on dealing with it. Over the next few weeks, we'll look at how and why He got into so much trouble for doing just that. As redeemed, forgiven people, let's also be joyful, shameless people. Happy Easter.

Optional further reading

Luke 24

The **label**

P ut yourself in Thomas' shoes. It's been quite a weekend. Your rabbi – your friend – has been brutally, publicly and very definitely crucified by the Romans. It's over. Jesus is dead and buried, and all the glorious reality of the last three years is fading so quickly you're starting to wonder if it even happened. Then your friends start trying to convince you that He's suddenly alive again. Is this a sick joke? Are they trying to upset you even more?

I'll believe it when I see it. Humanly speaking, Thomas' doubt seems pretty reasonable to me. Hope can be dangerous. If I were him, I'm not sure I'd have dared to believe something so wonderfully impossible. But here we are, two thousand years later, reading about an achingly relatable biblical figure who's been tarnished with shame throughout history: 'Doubting Thomas'. Imagine if your biggest failure, or even a temporary moment of doubt, became your name forever. One moment of very human rationalisation has the man labelled as a massive let-down with a legacy of 'a lack of faith', when in fact, his faith led him to a heroic martyr's death. People don't tend to die for their doubts, but still we've put Thomas in the Christian hall of shame instead of the hall of fame. Have you given yourself – or perhaps someone else – a shame prefix? 'Lazy.' 'Boring.' 'Cheating.' 'Stingy.' *Et cetera*.

We'll find out tomorrow how Jesus responded to Thomas' supposedly earth-shatteringly disappointing lack of faith. But for now, if there's a nickname or a reputation of shame hanging over you, know that you can reject it. Mocking never comes from Jesus.

John 20:24–25

'Unless I see the nail marks in his hands and put my finger where the nails were, and put my hand into his side, I will not believe.' (v25)

For prayer and reflection

Jesus, thank You that You don't label me by my mistakes and shortcomings. I bring all my doubts, worries and concerns to You today. Amen.

Asking for **help**

John 20:26–29

'Put your finger here; see my hands. Reach out your hand and put it into my side. Stop doubting and believe.' (v27)

I love that John specifies that these next events took place 'a week later' (v26), meaning Thomas had a full seven days to ruminate on all those Easter rumours and wrestle with his doubt. 'I'll believe it when I see it,' he'd effectively said. So, one week on, Jesus arrives (having walked through the walls, no less: 'Though the doors were locked, Jesus came and stood among them').

How does Jesus deal with Doubting Thomas? First of all, He comes in peace – not in anger, or disappointment, or chastisement. He doesn't criticise, shame or reprimand Thomas. He doesn't grab him by the shoulders and label him a failure, or even a doubter. Instead, He singles him out – His dear friend Thomas, who has been through a lot lately – and gives him exactly what he'd asked for: 'see my hands. Reach out your hand and put it into my side.' What a beautiful, quiet and kind gift.

For prayer and reflection

Jesus, thank You for meeting my shortcomings with so much kindness and grace. Help me to hear Your gentle, gracious and encouraging voice where I have perhaps imagined an angry one. Amen.

How do you imagine Jesus' voice sounds when He is speaking to Thomas here? Is He furious; fed up; rolling His eyes and sighing? Or is He smiling, reassuring and gentle? If this conversation took place today, perhaps He'd say, 'It's alright, Tom. I get it. It really is me... see for yourself.'

Believing the 'unbelievable' means we will occasionally (perhaps constantly) have questions. Do you think God is disappointed in you? Do you think He's angry with you because of your struggles, your doubts, your unbelief? Yes, we're called to 'faith without seeing', and Jesus says we will be blessed. But faith can be hard work. That's why we need His help with it. And here, Jesus gave Thomas some help.

What do you need help with today? Ask.

Unwavering

An extract from the introduction of Jen Baker's latest book

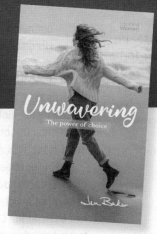

One of the most profound truths in the Bible is that regardless of how we came into this world – whether by love, passion or violence – we were chosen. God is intentional and at the moment of creation you were not only His first choice, but His best choice. At birth, He knew the number of hairs on your head (or lack thereof) and the number of days before you. God is responsible for bringing us into the world, but what we do with that time – and the legacy we choose to leave – is solely our responsibility.

Choice was created at the birth of Creation. The first Hebrew word of the Bible means 'in the beginning' and the second means God *(Elohim)*, with the third word, *bara*, meaning 'created'. Any type of creation, whether we are creating a meal or a memory, involves choice. Therefore, Elohim chose, before

time was established, to express His love by appointing mankind as the recipient of His love; because love without an object to love is unfulfilled, empty and void of purpose. In other words, *you* are God's desire!...

My prayer is that as you read, fear will lose its grip, faith will come alive, and purpose will be realigned… positioning you for a lifetime of relentless, kingdom pursuit.

This is your time, and this is your choice – make it an unwavering one.

Want to keep reading?
Visit **waverleyabbeyresources.org.uk/products/unwavering** to continue.

The **rock**

John 21:15–19;
Matthew 16:18

'Now I say to you
that you are Peter
(which means
"rock")'
(Matt. 16:18, NLT)

Continuing His post-resurrection reunion tour with
His disciples, Jesus stops by to see Peter.

Yes, *that* Peter. This could be awkward. By
some standards, perhaps we consider Peter's betrayal
of Jesus to be almost worse than Judas' – and his lack
of faith on the night of Jesus' arrest is arguably ten times
worse than Doubting Thomas' difficulty believing that
'dead Jesus' was now 'alive Jesus'.

But Jesus doesn't stop by to give a good old telling-
off to 'Peter the denying, backstabbing abandoner and
yellow-bellied chicken' – or even just jokingly reprimand
him as Peter the Coward, or Peter the Denier. He goes
to have a redemptive, heart-to-heart chat with His good
friend 'the Rock' (see Matt. 16:18), and puts his life back
on the right trajectory.* I've always found it interesting
that Peter gets away with such a glowing legacy,
despite being no less flawed than the others. (Aside: If
Judas Iscariot had stuck around, I wonder if he'd have
turned out to be Judas the Betrayer, or 'Judas who was
forgiven and went on to change the world'... we'll
never know.)

Jesus wasn't interested in reminding Peter of his
lowest and most shameful moment. He only wanted to
remind him of his identity, his purpose and his future.
Is this how we reach out to other people? Either we
believe that Jesus wipes the slate clean and gives us a
clean start, or we don't. If He does, surely that applies to
everyone, even if they've messed up in ways that make
us recoil in horror.

For prayer
and reflection

**Lord Jesus, if ever I
wrongly assume
that You think
badly of me,
remind me of who I
am in You. Thank
You again for what
You've done for me.
Amen.**

*If you're interested in reading more about Jesus' meeting with His disciples on
the beach, I recommend Jeff Lucas' book *Faith in the Fog* (Farnham: Waverley
Abbey Resources, 2020).

Redeeming the **dirt**

For the rest of the month, let's rewind a bit to before Jesus' arrest, and look at some examples from His ministry of how He dealt with the shame of those He encountered.

I'm first struck by the fact that Jesus *saw* this man, who was otherwise ignored by the rest of the world. He sees us even when we don't see Him. Notice, meanwhile, the disciples' assumptions that that this man was in some way responsible for having been born blind – that he or his parents must have sinned. It piles shame onto someone who's already suffering through no fault of their own, but it's easy still to think like this today. *Why is God punishing me?* We might prefer this way of thinking because it lets us believe there's a balance to be restored that's within our control; a wrong to be righted; a 'why', when really things are often devastating, disappointing or just plain difficult for no apparent reason. (Job's friends seemed to struggle to grasp this too.) Jesus didn't try to explain away this man's suffering – He was simply willing to do something amazing with it.

Then, instead of reaching for an elaborate medical formula (as amazing as those can be), He bent down in the dirt... and spat.

This is the Messiah who uses the foolish things of the world to shame the wise (1 Cor. 1:27). How many people had spat on this man as he scraped a living in the dirt for all those years? But along comes Jesus, who uses what had been a way of keeping this man low, shamed and isolated, to restore him. It's as if He says, 'I will use this mud and spit and turn it into the best story you'll ever tell.'

> **John 9:1–7;**
> **1 Corinthians**
> **1:27**
>
> 'After saying this, he spat on the ground, made some mud with the saliva, and put it on the man's eyes.'
> (John 9:6)

The **guest** of a **sinner**

Luke 19:1–9

'All the people saw this and began to mutter, "He has gone to be the guest of a sinner."' (v7)

While the blind man we read about yesterday had done nothing to bring about his own suffering, human behaviour generally has consequences. We might be inclined to avoid someone not because they're a bit strange or different or 'needy' in ways we'd rather not rise to, but because they have actively hurt people. Zacchaeus wasn't a popular guy. He'd taken advantage of his professional position and done quite well out of trampling on other people. Yet this is the man who caught Jesus' eye that day – not the exploited, but the exploiter. Both matter to Him.

The crowd noticed Jesus' inclusion of sinners, and muttered that He was hanging out with the 'wrong sorts' of people. Sometimes these reputations were because they were cut from the wrong cloth (in the eyes of society), while others made their own mess. Perhaps we're not overly offended by tax collectors in this day and age, but it's likely we've all been the mutterers at some point – especially if we know of Christians who associate with people we don't approve of. Jesus wanted to have dinner with Zacchaeus *before* he had cleaned up his act, but do we expect people to change their beliefs and behaviour before they belong in our churches?

We know that Zacchaeus was up in the tree primarily because of a height disadvantage (v3), but perhaps it also symbolised his sense of shame and social isolation. Jesus saw right to the heart of the matter, and responded by treating him like a human being and a friend. From that point, Zacchaeus was able to acknowledge his guilt of his own accord – and make the changes needed in order to put things right and live differently.

For prayer and reflection

God, help me not to be judgmental of others, but to see them as You do and accept them as they are. Amen.

Weekend

Shameless hope

....

Romans 5:1–11

'And hope does not put us to shame, because God's love has been poured out into our hearts through the Holy Spirit' (v5)

We'll continue our weekends reflecting on some New Testament ideas about living a shame-free life.

Despite writing under intense persecution, Paul was able to keep hope – specifically hope in Jesus – at the heart of his letter to the Romans. The NIV translates this verse with the word 'shame', though most others seem to use 'disappointment' (or similar). The hope we have in Jesus will *never* disappoint us.

Paul was able to speak straight to the hearts of those experiencing religious persecution because, rather uniquely, he knew what it was to be on both sides of it. But even though he'd been pretty successful at being a zealous, Christian-persecuting Jew, Paul (then Saul) clearly hadn't found what he'd been looking for… until he met Jesus. He'd done some pretty shameful things in his past – things that may have shaped him, but now no longer shamed him, and actually made him a very effective evangelist.

In life, you may occasionally face ridicule for your faith, but don't let it hold you back. Make it a part of your story. Hope does not put us to shame.

....

Optional further reading

John 16:33

The first **stone**

John 8:1–8

'Let any one of you who is without sin be the first to throw a stone at her.' (v7)

T his week, let's take a look at a couple of different women whose lives were utterly transformed when Jesus freed them from shame. First: the woman caught in adultery.

The words 'caught in adultery' might go straight over your head, but consider for a moment what that probably meant. She was caught *in the act*. How humiliating! Was she given the chance to get dressed before being dragged from the house? We're not told (just as we don't know if the man she was caught with was held to the same standard), but 'They made her stand before the group' (v3). Everyone knew what she had done, and where this was likely going.

This woman was a pawn in the Pharisees' plan to theologically corner Jesus into condemning her, but it backfired somewhat. Instead, He irrefutably evicted them from the moral high ground. We don't know what Jesus wrote in the dirt, but one possibility is that He called out some of their sins, some of which perhaps included adultery and other 'stoning-worthy' offences. The only person without sin, the *only* person who could throw the first stone was, is and ever will be Jesus – and He didn't.

The late Rachel Held Evans, one of my favourite authors, took the life and death of Jesus as a sign that 'God would rather die by violence than commit it.'* Jesus didn't throw the stone. Some time later, He Himself, half-naked and humiliated, would be brought before a clown court of Pharisees, while the crowd called for His execution. I like to think He thought of this woman at that moment.

*Rachel Held Evans, *Inspired* (Nashville, TN, USA: Nelson Books, 2018)

For prayer and reflection

Shockingly, execution by stoning is still practised in some parts of the world today. Spend some time praying and interceding for this issue now.

Where are they?

John 8:9–11

'Jesus straightened up and asked her, "Woman, where are they? Has no one condemned you?"' (v10)

Imagine the anger, tension and resignation in the air as the dumbfounded Pharisees began to drop their stones and slope off, one by one. What a glorious 'I rest my case' moment. Soon, there was no one left except for the woman and Jesus. It's not possible for her life to have changed direction more radically than it did in those few minutes. I can imagine her disbelief; her embarrassment; her elation; her confusion; her gratitude; her joy. There was no one left to condemn her. When our shame collides with the shameless love of Jesus, we get the gospel.

So, what next? How was this woman to respond to what had just happened? Though Jesus never brought charges against her, her guilt would hardly have needed expounding any further. We don't know the circumstances surrounding the adultery, but Jesus telling her to leave her life of sin (v11) does indicate that she had some responsibility, however unequal relationships might have been in that culture. She had been shown unprecedented forgiveness, and now she was to make a choice to move forward. A behavioural change would be involved, but it wouldn't necessarily have to be complicated – simply Jesus' 'I forgive you... just don't do it anymore.' And there's no limit on how many times we get offered this. That's what grace is.

If you feel like you're standing in front of a crowd of 'accusers' today, whatever that might look like, let Jesus be your defence. He's on excellent terms with the Judge. And one day, you'll get to stand before Him and have Him ask you, 'Where are your accusers?', and no one will condemn you. Neither will He.

For prayer and reflection

Jesus, even when my guilt is so obvious, I thank You that You don't condemn me. Help me to leave behind any self-destructive behaviour I might be struggling with today. Amen.

Are you talking **to me?**

'The Samaritan woman said to him, "You are a Jew and I am a Samaritan woman. How can you ask me for a drink?" (For Jews do not associate with Samaritans.)' (v9)

It's hard to imagine a world without division and segregation, and it's not a new problem. A lot of the cultural nuances referred to in the Gospels are lost on us today, but they certainly would have been shocking at the time. For example: Jewish men did not speak to women. Jews did not speak to Samaritans. Jewish men therefore most definitely did not speak to Samaritan women.

We've come a long way, but if you've ever been ignored because you are a woman, this is a beautiful picture for you: here is Jesus, completely disregarding any of the social, cultural or religious conventions that might stop Him from talking to this woman. He couldn't break any more etiquette here if He tried. That brings such a huge smile to my face. Nothing can ever stop Him wanting to have a conversation with me. He isn't embarrassed by me, or ashamed to be seen with me, or even associated with me. He never gives me the brush-off, or pretends not to have heard me. If I'm completely honest, though, I can't always swap 'He' and 'me' in those sentences with the same degree of ease or even truth – but I'm working on it.

Are there any social conventions impeding the ways in which you reach out to people? While she was preaching a few years ago, a friend of mine said this: 'You will never look into the eyes of someone who isn't totally loved and adored by Jesus.' While it's important to be sensitive and respectful of other people's customs, let's make sure that's the thing we remember, and ask for boldness as well as wisdom. We might be the only person they meet who knows Jesus.

For prayer and reflection

Lord, help me to see people as You see them, and look for the gold in them. Give me wisdom and boldness in my conversations with people who don't yet know You. Amen.

Waverley Abbey College

Education that changes lives

Our programmes equip students with the skills and knowledge to release their God-given potential to operate in roles that help people.

Central to all of our teaching is the Waverley Integrative Framework. Built on 50 years of experience, the model emphasises the importance of genuineness, unconditional acceptance and empathy in relationships. The courses we offer range from certificates to Higher Education level.

Counselling

As society begins to realise the extent of its brokenness, we continue to recognise the need to train people to support those who are struggling with everyday life, providing training to equip individuals to become professional counsellors. Whatever their starting point in academic learning, we have a pathway to help all students on their academic journey.

Spiritual Formation

For those wanting to be better equipped to help others on their spiritual journey, this programme provides robust and effective Spiritual Formation training. Students engage with theology, psychology, social sciences, historical studies, counselling, leadership studies and psychotherapy.

For more information about all of our course offerings available, visit **waverleyabbeycollege.ac.uk**

What's **really** going on?

John 4:16–26

'I have no husband,' she replied. Jesus said to her, 'You are right when you say you have no husband.'" (v17)

I find the dynamics of this conversation really interesting. While the Samaritan woman is intrigued, she doesn't seem intimidated: Jesus clearly isn't the first man she's ever spoken to. But He's probably the first to treat her with this level of dignity and respect. In today's verses, He even appears to be bantering with her a bit: 'Go, call your husband and come back' (v16).

Was He trying to make her blush, or feel ashamed of her sexual history? I would strongly argue that that's not what's happening here. I imagine Jesus had a twinkle in His eye when He asked this, knowing it would lead to a much more important conversation that would actually win over her trust in Him. When God asked Adam and Eve, 'Where are you?' after the Fall (Gen. 3), it wasn't because He didn't know. He was inviting them to talk to Him about what was really going on.

Just as with the woman caught in adultery we read about earlier this week (see John 8), Jesus was able to demonstrate His intimate knowledge of this woman's life and heart without rejection, judgment or shame. Despite her relationship status and her culture, she would not be disqualified from the salvation that was coming.

Sexuality and sexual history can be an area of shame for a lot of people (arguably women in particular, given the double standards still prevalent in society), and in some cases this may even have been exacerbated by what has been taught in church. But whatever you think makes you not good enough, Jesus knows about it anyway, and still wants to talk with you. He invites you to simply speak to Him about what's really going on in your life.

For prayer and reflection

Jesus, even though You already know the whole story, help me to be really honest and vulnerable with You when I pray. Thank You for taking me exactly as You find me. Amen.

No question

I've never noticed this part of the Bible before, but it's fast becoming one of my favourites. Nobody questioned why Jesus was talking with this woman. Yes, they were surprised. But I like to think the disciples were learning not to question Jesus' shameless dismantling of the gender apartheid in that culture.

Without 'man-bashing' in any way, or imagining there to be persecution where there may be none, I want to borrow these words of activist Dorothy Day, because I think they so beautifully encapsulate Jesus' heart:

'Perhaps it is no wonder that the women were first at the Cradle and last at the Cross. They had never known a man like this Man—there never has been another. A prophet and teacher who never nagged at them, never flattered or coaxed or patronized; who never made arch jokes about them, never treated them as "The women, God help us!" or "The ladies, God bless them!"; who rebuked without querulousness and praised without condescension; who took their questions and arguments seriously; who never mapped out their sphere for them, never urged them to be feminine or jeered at them for being female; who had no axe to grind and no uneasy male dignity to defend; who took them as he found them and was completely unselfconscious. There is no act, no sermon, no parable in the whole Gospel that borrows its pungency from female perversity; nobody could guess from the words and deeds of Jesus that there was anything "funny" about woman's nature.'

Jesus loves women. He has absolutely no interest in holding you back, belittling or excluding you. Quite the opposite. I hope that encourages you today.

*Dorothy Day, cited by Sarah Bessey in *Jesus Feminist*
(New York: Howard Books, 2013)

John 4:27–30

'Just then his disciples returned and were surprised to find him talking with a woman. But no one asked, "What do you want?" or "Why are you talking with her?"' (v27)

For prayer and reflection

Have you ever faced exclusion or disqualification because of the fact that you're a woman? Spend some time in God's presence and ask Him to bring healing if and where it is needed.

The best story wins

....

Romans 1:16–17

'For I am not ashamed of the gospel, because it is the power of God that brings salvation to everyone who believes' (v16)

As we look at so many stories of people in the Bible whose lives were touched by Jesus, I can't help but be struck by how 'the gospel' meant something different for each of them. All of these encounters were uniquely personal to the people involved, and the good news of Jesus looked slightly different for each person – whether it was the dismantling of a divisive social paradigm, smashing through cultural barriers, a stigma removed, a death sentence repealed, a new lease of life, health restored, or a destiny revealed. It's all good news.

Storytelling consultant Bobette Buster writes, 'Narrative is our culture's currency. He who tells the best story wins.'* You have the best story to tell, because you've been written into God's. How you have encountered Jesus, and how He has changed your life, is unique to you.

Paul was not ashamed of the story he had to tell, even though it might mean persecution, perhaps to the point of death. This weekend, think of the people that you long to see get to know Jesus and get written into this amazing story. What might it look like for them?

*Bobette Buster, *Do Story: How to tell your story so the world listens* (San Francisco: Chronicle Books, 2018)

....

Optional further reading

Ephesians 1:3–14; 1 Peter 3:15

Get out of the **kitchen**

Luke 10:38–42

Just as the world-changing disciple Thomas has been labelled by his doubt, people seem to remember Martha for being far too busy to worship Jesus as He really deserved. But is that fair? Is that what Jesus thought?

Whenever we have guests over, I'm usually the one in the kitchen getting everyone's drinks, occasionally yelling for an extra pair of hands while my husband is kicking back with our guests in the lounge. I want people to feel welcome in our home, and my hospitality often manifests as service, while Chris is amazingly personable. It's not at all hard for me to relate to Martha's frustration. (As an aside, we read in verse 40 that Martha was 'distracted by the preparations that had to be made' – the kitchen isn't even mentioned.) It seems to me that Martha is often unfairly criticised for what many of us would also most likely do in her situation.

Now consider Jesus' response to her. There is no telling-off – so let's not read a reprimand into the scene when what Jesus is really saying is, 'Don't worry about all that. Come and sit with me.' Let's not hear an angry and disappointed Jesus when we've got a kind, empathetic and gentle Jesus who invites women to spend time with Him just as his male disciples would. In those days, Jewish women simply did not sit at the feet of rabbis. (Girls weren't even taught the Torah.) So for Jesus to invite Martha and Mary to do just that is radically inclusive.

Based on this passage, if you've got any questions about 'a woman's place', here it is: at the feet of Jesus, learning as a disciple... not necessarily in the kitchen.

'Martha, Martha... you are worried and upset about many things, but few things are needed – or indeed only one.' (vv41–42)

For prayer and reflection

Jesus, help me to remember that the highest calling placed on my life is to be Your disciple. Help me not to confuse working *for* You and working *with* You. Amen.

An eclectic **guestlist**

Luke 15:1–2

'This man welcomes sinners, and eats with them.' (v2)

Have you ever played the dinner party game? Hypothetically, you're allowed to invite anyone you like, whether dead or alive, to your dream dinner party. For the dynamics and the banter, I'd probably keep things girls-only and suggest names like Michelle Obama, Jane Austen, Judi Dench, Ruth Bader Ginsburg, Rachel Held Evans, Celeste Barber, Jacinda Ardern, Aretha Franklin... I'd choose 'inspiring women' – funny, articulate creatives, revolutionaries and history-makers. Jesus apparently had very different criteria: He'd have dinner with the people no one else wanted at theirs. I'd invite the brilliant people; Jesus would invite the broken people.

Before we spend a couple of days looking at the parable of the prodigal son (which perhaps has more shame-busting crammed into it than any other story told by Jesus), let's first consider these two short verses that come not long before: 'Now the tax collectors and sinners were all gathering round to hear Jesus. But the Pharisees and the teachers of the law muttered, "This man welcomes sinners, and eats with them."'

In that culture, eating with someone was a significant gesture of acceptance, and according to religious law, eating with a 'sinner' would make you 'unclean'. No wonder Jesus confused the legalistic religious elite. He wasn't afraid to associate with despised, rejected, frowned-upon people. He wasn't at all ashamed to be seen with them. This was the audience to which Jesus would tell His parables of being lost and found: a rabble of assorted misfits, and a muttering herd of self-righteous Pharisees. Quite the crowd...

For prayer and reflection

God, challenge me on the criteria by which I evaluate people. Help me to be as loving, inclusive and generous with my life as You would want me to be. Amen.

The **running** father

I like to think of this as a double-edged shame-busting parable (Jesus told stories with imagery that would drive His point home, loud and clear). While we might prefer to focus on the riches-to-rags descent of the selfish and debauched younger son, what would have been most difficult for the listening Pharisees to stomach was the 'shameful' behaviour of the father. A righteous and respectable man would *not* be seen running in public, skirts round his ankles, shouting with love for his wayward son. This parable says more about God than it does about us.

Artist Charlie Mackesy, now well-known for his sketches on Instagram, has also created several beautiful drawings and sculptures inspired by this parable. Handwritten over his painting known as 'The Prodigal Daughter' are these words: 'This is the story of the prodigal daughter – It should really be called the running Father who waited every day for his girl to come home – the daughter who had rejected him so badly – but when he saw her from a long way off – he ran to her and hugged her and kissed her'.

God doesn't seem to prioritise His 'dignity' in the lengths He goes to show us how much He loves us. Jesus' coming to earth and being born to a teenage refugee couple in an outbuilding wasn't especially dignified, but that was how He did it. God having to live in a human body (and all that goes with it) would have had moments we might not consider to be particularly dignified. Crucifixion was deliberately as undignified a death as humanly possible. His love is shameless. He is the running Father.

Luke 15:11–31

'But while he was still a long way off, his father saw him and was filled with compassion for him; he ran to his son, threw his arms round him and kissed him.' (v20)

For prayer and reflection

Father God, if ever I'm hesitant about coming back to You, help me to remember that You run out to meet me. Thank You for always welcoming me home. Amen.

Making **a point**

Luke 15:11–31

'So he went and hired himself out to a citizen of that country, who sent him to his fields to feed pigs.' (v15)

As we touched on yesterday, Jesus' parables were designed to teach. The details mattered, even though some of them are a bit lost on us today. Judging by the crowds that followed Him and gathered to hear Him speak, Jesus was a very effective communicator and no doubt a captivating storyteller. He probably told this story in such a way that would make some of His audience tut-tut at the actions of the characters.

Picking up on just a few of these things: first, there's the insult of the son asking his living father for his inheritance early. This wasn't a million miles from saying, 'I wish you were dead.' Then, there's how he spent it: on self-destructive behaviour, partying hard, bad habits, bad company and bad ideas. Before hitting rock-bottom, this son of a respected and prosperous man found himself working as an immigrant labourer, until he finally ended up as the servant of pigs. Yes, pigs – pretty much as 'unclean' as it got. From a cultural perspective, Jesus probably couldn't cram much more offensive, unclean material in this parable if He tried. And as soon as He'd set the scene, grace and forgiveness invaded the story like a mop and a bucket of bleach.

If Jesus were to tell you a parable today, what details would make it truly offensive or disgusting to you? Would it feature a sex offender; a terrorist; a racist police officer; a corrupt judge? The point is, the gospel is offensive to some people. There isn't really a hierarchy of sin, where some people are worse than others. We're all in the same boat. Perhaps that's why the Pharisees struggled the most to accept that they needed a Saviour.

For prayer and reflection

Jesus, keep me humble if I ever edge towards self-righteousness. When I'm offended by something, help me to really think about why, and look at my own life. Amen.

Next Issue

MAY/JUN 2021

May

THE 'YES'S' OF GOD

RACHEL WRIGHT

June

THE SACRED EVERYDAY

ELISABETH PIKE

Also available as
eBook/eSubscription

In **May**, Rachel Wright looks at the 'Yes's' of the Bible and how, despite the temptation to tie ourselves up with 'no's, God is about more, rather than less; freedom, rather than restriction.

In **June**, Elisabeth Pike encourages us to stay in tune with the holy, opening our eyes to God's presence with us every day and viewing even what seems to be mundane as sacred.

Obtain your copy from Waverley Abbey Resources, Christian bookshops or your National Distributor. If you would like to take out a subscription, see the order form at the back of these notes.

I am **willing**

**Leviticus
13:45–46;
Matthew 8:1–4**

'Jesus reached out
his hand and
touched the man.
"I am willing," he
said. "Be clean!"
Immediately he
was cleansed of
his leprosy.'
(Matt. 8:3)

Considered by the World Health Organisation to be officially eliminated for over 20 years now, it's hard for us to grasp how devastating leprosy, a totally curable disease today, would have been for sufferers two thousand years ago. Lepers were expected to live in isolation, separated from their communities, and announce their condition to anyone near them by shouting, 'Unclean!'

Surely speaking 'unclean' over themselves so often is going to make it hard for a person to believe anything else. That's the power of shame. Imagine having to broadcast your private medical details, your secrets, your regrets – anything that might bring you disgrace or embarrassment. What 'unclean' statements do you make over yourself? 'I am damaged goods.' 'I am not enough.' 'I am not worthy of love.' 'I am not a good friend/employee/mother.' 'I am a disappointment.' 'I am mediocre.' 'I am ugly.'

Jesus' response to the leper in this story is simply: 'I am willing.' He effectively says, 'Be clean. Be who I say you are.' Despite the fact that reaching out and touching a person with leprosy would have made Him ceremonially unclean, Jesus was willing to smash through yet another social and religious barrier in order to directly address the physical causes and effects of this man's shame and isolation.

Jesus is not weird about human bodies. He didn't mind having one; He didn't mind touching dead bodies to resurrect them, or reaching out to infected ones to heal them. He designed us to live in them. Whatever damage, injury or decay our bodies might have suffered – or caused – God is willing to come close to us.

**For prayer
and reflection**

**Jesus, thank You
that You are
always willing to
cleanse, redeem
and restore. If ever
I assume that
whatever I've done
or experienced
makes me
repulsive to You,
remind me who
You are. Amen.**

Children of God

....

1 John 3:1–3

'See what great love the Father has lavished on us, that we should be called children of God! And that is what we are!' (v1)

Shame researcher Brené Brown (yes, that really is her job) said, 'Those who have a strong sense of love and belonging have the courage to be imperfect.' As children of God, we know we are loved and we know we belong to Him. It seems to me that one of Jesus' top priorities was showing people that they were loved and that they were welcome; they belonged. The fact that they were imperfect wasn't really an issue, because they were human. Jesus doesn't ask for perfect, because *He* is perfect. Perfectionism provides the perfect breeding ground for shame and disappointment.

If we're to show God's love to the world in a way it understands, we need to remember that mucky children are no less loveable to their parents. Sick children are no less loveable. Neglected and abused children are no less loveable. Spoiled and indulged children are no less worthy of love. Naughty children will perhaps temporarily incur frustration, anger and even fear (humanly speaking), but to a caring parent, those children are no less loved.

What does it mean to you to be a child of God?

....

Optional further reading
Christine Caine, *Unashamed* (Grand Rapids, MI, USA: Zondervan, 2016)

Just a **touch**

Mark 5:21–34

'Then the woman… fell at his feet and, trembling with fear, told him the whole truth.' (v33)

L adies: I like to think that we're getting better at talking about things like puberty, menstruation, (in)fertility, pregnancy and menopause as normal and factual parts of our lives – all of which can also come with huge challenges. I'm blessed that my husband can handle my frankness when I need to talk to him about 'women's things', and he's able to show his support without embarrassment.

I can only imagine the shame, desperation and fear of this woman who had endured the physical and emotional pain of a 12-year bleed, let alone her loneliness and social isolation (have a quick read of Leviticus 15:19–30, and thank God that those rules no longer apply). Perhaps she took extra measures to try to disguise her condition as she contended with enormous crowds just to get a glimpse of the Jesus who could heal her. So now consider her shock and relief at Jesus' response when, 'trembling with fear, [she] told him the whole truth' (v33). Jesus wasn't disgusted by her, or even remotely flustered. Yes, He noticed that He had been touched with intention amidst a heaving crowd, but there's nothing to suggest that He was horrified – only intrigued. And He healed and blessed her.

Just as with the leper we read about on Friday, Jesus wasn't offended by this woman's human body. In fact, this incident comes almost as an interruption to His healing a young girl, whom He later resurrects (by touching her dead body). This was a lot of 'uncleanness' for Jesus to be coming into contact with for just one day, but He didn't seem to mind. He is so pure and so holy that our stains just don't stick to Him. They're blotted out in an instant.

For prayer and reflection

Jesus, thank You that You see me and hear me, no matter who else is in need of Your attention. Help me to approach You with faith and boldness. Amen.

A shameless **display**

Luke 7:36–50

J esus regularly ate with the riff-raff, but He also ate with the Pharisees when He was invited (v36), so it's not as if what He was offering was off-limits to them. He offered them the same opportunities as He did everyone else… it's just that they had a bit more difficulty grasping His message.

'If this man were a prophet, he would know who is touching him and what kind of woman she is' (v39)

There's so much we could pull out from this story, but I'd like to focus on this woman's shameless act of worship to Jesus. Despite all the supposedly righteous men watching, she wasn't afraid to bring all her baggage into the room and leave it at His feet. She understood the power of the forgiveness that was available to her. She wasn't ashamed of her love for Jesus.

Simon's rebuke of her display (which, admittedly, does seem quite dramatic), whether said out loud or 'to himself' (v39), did not go unheard by Jesus. This 'kind of woman' was 'a sinner', just as 100% of people are – not that the Pharisees seemed to get that! Perhaps we naturally assume that her sin must have been sexual in some way, and therefore worse or more disgraceful by some totally arbitrary standard. Whatever the Pharisees thought of her, they certainly didn't consider her welcome.

Jesus asks Simon, 'Do you see this woman?' As I read that, I naturally place an emphasis on 'see'. He *sees* her – not least because He isn't afraid to look at her. He doesn't turn His face away. Instead He turns towards her, sees her shameless outpouring of love and says, 'You see this? Beautiful, isn't it?' When we worship God without fear, and in Spirit and in truth (John 4:23), our love is never received by Him with condescension, disapproval or disgust.

For prayer and reflection

Lord, help me to be brave and unembarrassed in my worship of You. Help me to understand the power of the forgiveness that is available to me. Amen.

A **glutton** and a **drunkard**

**Matthew
11:18–19**

'Here is a glutton
and a drunkard, a
friend of tax
collectors and
sinners.' (v19)

I love that while God was on earth in the form of Jesus, He got into enough trouble to get a bad reputation among the religious busybodies. Here, He's calling out the Pharisees for being so cynical. They criticised John the Baptist for being too self-denying, while they accused Jesus of hanging with the wrong crowd and having being too self-indulgent. Their standards were impossible. With their warped perception of perfectionism, everyone fell short – even Jesus. A pharisaic outlook on life is a breeding ground for shame.

The danger of religion is that it often declares things bad that are meant to be good. Jesus was fun and got invited to parties. He made people feel seen and valued and brought joy and great enrichment to their lives. He improved things for people everywhere He went. He laughed. He celebrated. He rested. He ate and drank and socialised. He told stories, and probably jokes. He went to great lengths to show the unworthy that they are precious in His sight, and modelled this way of living to His followers. As Rachel Held Evans puts it so beautifully: 'The apostles remembered what many modern Christians tend to forget—that what makes the gospel offensive isn't who it keeps out but who it lets in.'*

If you were to paint a picture of Jesus now, how would you draw Him? Smiling? Laughing? Embracing? Eating? Reclining with a glass of wine? Playing with the kids, or messing around in boats with His disciples? That's the Jesus I want to reflect to the world. Focused, courageous and generous with my life, yes – but also interruptible, welcoming and fun.

*Rachel Held Evans, *Inspired*, Nashville, TN, USA: Nelson Books, 2018)

**For prayer
and reflection**

**God, You are fun!
Help me to be
unafraid to have
fun, and not to let
shame or religion
stop me from
enjoying my life
with You. Amen.**

Taking **a stand**

When we've spent most of this month looking at Jesus' quiet, revolutionary ways (significant as they were), it feels a bit strange now to look at a couple of examples of Him making a bit more noise. Our God is not shy when it comes to justice, and nor should we be.

We see these two passionate outbursts from Jesus when those responsible for leading people spiritually are doing so in totally the wrong direction. The Pharisees, the money lenders – they were misrepresenting what a life and relationship with God should look like. Jesus came to turn the tables, quite literally.

It's interesting that the firmest rebukes we read of Jesus giving are aimed at the religious leaders who had wilfully grabbed the wrong end of the stick, using their religious rules and impossible standards to exploit people and set them up to fail. I think there's little that upsets God more than people doing things in His name that go against His character. (This is where the Church has often gone wrong throughout history: monarchs, nations and leaders with their own agendas; wars and crusades taking place in the name of religion; Scripture taken out of context and used to defend slavery, discrimination and greed.) Perhaps that's what 'taking the Lord's name in vain' really means – misusing it as a weapon to justify all the wrong things.

Jesus knew how to take a stand for what was right - and what He stood up for *was* definitely right. If we're going to courageously take a stand for something in the name of Jesus, let's be sure that He would too. He loved the Pharisees, but they seemed to frustrate Him more than anybody else.

Matthew 21:12 13; 23:27–28

'on the outside you appear to people as righteous but on the inside you are full of hypocrisy and wickedness.' (Matt. 23:28)

For prayer and reflection

Lord, give me Your heart for justice. Bring to my attention the issues that really matter, and help me to take a stand that honours You and other people. Amen.

With **confidence**

**Hebrews
4:14–16**

'Let us then approach God's throne of grace with confidence, so that we may receive mercy and find grace to help us in our time of need.' (v16)

We've all heard people joking about how they'd 'better not go inside a church', just in case they 'catch fire'. I can't help wondering how many more people might take a chance on church if they were confident that they wouldn't be rejected, excluded, or expected to change who they are overnight. If people really knew the welcome they would get from Jesus, would they, like the Samaritan woman, the bleeding woman or the leper, then feel able to look Him in the eye?

Maybe approaching 'God's throne of grace' is not something you've ever felt able to do with confidence. Maybe you're inclined to avoid holy places (literally or metaphorically) out of fear that you're not good enough, or will be somehow turned away. If there's anything we can learn from the stories we've been reading – from the encounters that people had with Jesus – it's that while He deserves our reverence and awe, He's also totally approachable; loving; friendly; kind. We are in the safest hands. Jesus left the throne of heaven to come and show people just how acceptable to Him they are.

I love how *The Message* translates these verses from Hebrews, and they brilliantly summarise how we can shamelessly approach our shameless Jesus and receive from Him everything we need:

'Now that we know what we have—Jesus, this great High Priest with ready access to God—let's not let it slip through our fingers. We don't have a priest who is out of touch with our reality. He's been through weakness and testing, experienced it all—all but the sin. So let's walk right up to him and get what he is so ready to give. Take the mercy, accept the help.'

**For prayer
and reflection**

Jesus, thank You for who You are. I want to walk right up to You and receive what You are so ready to give me. Amen.

Order form

IWED M/A 2021

Get Your **FREE** Daily Bible Reading Notes **TODAY!** (UK ONLY)

From January 2021 your favourite Bible Reading notes will be available to you for FREE. God has called us back to the original vision of CWR to provide these notes to everyone who needs them, regardless of their circumstance or ability to pay. It is our desire to see these daily bible reading notes used more widely, to see Christians grow in their relationship with Jesus on a daily basis and to see Him reflected in their everyday living. More than 60,000 copies each year are delivered into prisons too and our vision is to grow this ministry even further, putting these notes into the hands of those in challenging situations and to see their lives transformed through a new and growing relationship with Jesus. Clearly there are costs to provide this ministry and we are trusting in God's provision.

Could you be part of this vision? Do you have the desire to see lives transformed through a relationship with Jesus? **A small donation from you of just £2 a month, by direct debit, will make such a difference** Giving hope to someone in desperate need whilst you too grow deeper in your own relationship with Jesus.

4 Easy Ways To Order

1. Visit our online store at **waverleyabbeyresources.org/store**
2. Send this form together with your payment to: **CWR, Waverley Abbey House, Waverley Lane, Farnham, Surrey GU9 8EP**
3. Phone in your credit card order: **01252 784700** (Mon–Fri, 9.30am – 4.30pm)
4. Visit a Christian bookshop

For a list of our National Distributors, who supply countries outside the UK, visit waverleyabbeyresources.org/distributors

Your Details (required for orders and donations)

Full Name:	CWR ID No. (if known):
Home Address:	
	Postcode:
Telephone No. (for queries):	Email:

Publications

TITLE	QTY	PRICE	TOTAL
		TOTAL PUBLICATIONS	

UK P&P: up to £24.99 = **£2.99**; £25.00 and over = **FREE**

Elsewhere P&P: up to £10 = **£4.95**; £10.01 – £50 = **£6.95**; £50.01 – £99.99 = **£10**; £100 and over = **£30**

Total Publications and P&P (please allow 14 days for delivery)	**A**	

Payment Details

☐ I enclose a cheque made payable to CWR for the amount of: **£** _____

☐ Please charge my credit/debit card.

Cardholder's Name (in BLOCK CAPITALS) _____

Card No. ☐☐☐☐ ☐☐☐☐ ☐☐☐☐ ☐☐☐☐

Expires End ☐☐ ☐☐   Security Code ☐☐☐

Continued overleaf >>

One off Special Gift to CWR ☐ Please send me an acknowledgement of my gift **B**

GRAND TOTAL (Total of A & B)

Gift Aid (your home address required, see overleaf)

giftaid it I am a UK taxpayer and want CWR to reclaim the tax on all my donations for the four years prior to this year **and on** all donations I make from the date of this Gift Aid declaration until further notice.*

Taxpayer's Full Name (in BLOCK CAPITALS) _____

Signature _____ **Date** _____

*I am a UK taxpayer and understand that if I pay less Income Tax and/or Capital Gains Tax than the amount of Gift Aid claimed on all my donations in that tax year it is my responsibility to pay any difference.

Your FREE Daily Bible Reading Notes Order

	Please Tick	FREE	£2 pcm	£5 pcm	£10 pcm	Other
Every Day with Jesus		☐	☐	☐	☐	☐ £ ___
Large Print *Every Day with Jesus*		☐	☐	☐	☐	☐ £ ___
Inspiring Women Every Day		☐	☐	☐	☐	☐ £ ___

All CWR Bible reading notes are also available in single issue **ebook** and **email subscription** format. Visit **waverleyabbeyresources.org** for further info.

CWR Instruction to your Bank or Building Society to pay by Direct Debit

Please fill in the form and send to: CWR, Waverley Abbey House, Waverley Lane, Farnham, Surrey GU9 8EP

DIRECT Debit

Name and full postal address of your Bank or Building Society

To: The Manager   Bank/Building Society

Address

_____

_____

Postcode

Name(s) of Account Holder(s)

Branch Sort Code

Bank/Building Society Account Number

Originator's Identification Number

4	2	0	4	8	7

Reference

Instruction to your Bank or Building Society

Please pay CWR Direct Debits from the account detailed in this Instruc subject to the safeguards assured by the Direct Debit Guarantee. I understand that this Instruction may remain with CWR and, if so, detail will be passed electronically to my Bank/Building Society.

Signature(s)

Date

Banks and Building Societies may not accept Direct Debit Instructions for some types of account

---

For a subscription outside of the UK please visit www.waverleyabbeyresources.org where you will find a list of our national distributors.

How would you like to hear from us? We would love to keep you up to date on all aspects of the CWR ministry, including; new publications, events & courses as well as how you can support us.

If you **DO** want to hear from us on email, please tick here [ ] If you **DO NOT** want us to contact you by post, please tick here

You can update your preferences at any time by contacting our customer services team on 01252 784 700. You can view our privacy policy online at waverleyabbeyresources.org